RAND INTERNATIONAL

Youth in Jordan

Transitions from Education to Employment

Ryan Andrew Brown, Louay Constant, Peter Glick, Audra K. Grant

Prepared for the Center for Middle East Public Policy

The research described in this report was sponsored by the RAND Initiative for Middle Eastern Youth and conducted within the RAND Center for Middle East Public Policy, part of International Programs at the RAND Corporation. CMEPP brings together analytic excellence and regional expertise from across the RAND Corporation to address the most critical political, social, and economic challenges facing the Middle East today.

Library of Congress Control Number: 2014940276

ISBN: 978-0-8330-8687-7

Preface

The research described in this report was sponsored by the RAND Initiative for Middle Eastern Youth and conducted within the RAND Center for Middle East Public Policy, part of International Programs at the RAND Corporation. CMEPP brings together analytic excellence and regional expertise from across the RAND Corporation to address the most critical political, social, and economic challenges facing the Middle East today. The RAND Corporation is a nonprofit institution that helps improve policy and decisionmaking through research and analysis. RAND focuses on the issues that matter most, such as health, education, national security, international affairs, law and business, and the environment. RAND's work on the Middle East is conducted by virtually every one of its many research units. CMEPP is the mechanism by which RAND's experts on economics, health, education, and national security research are paired with its experts on the political, societal, and cultural issues in the region. In this way, RAND is able to bring to bear a full array of analytic capabilities to understand the Middle East in the broadest possible sense.

For more information on this report, contact Peter Glick. He can be reached by email at Peter_Glick@rand.org; by phone at 703-413-1100, x5426; or by mail at the RAND Corporation, 1200 South Hayes Street, Arlington, VA 22202-5050.

For more information on CMEPP, contact Dalia Dassa Kaye, Director, Center for Middle East Public Policy, RAND Corporation, 1776 Main Street, P.O. Box 2138, Santa Monica, CA 90407-2138, 310-393-0411, x6118, Dalia_Kaye@rand.org.

Contents

Figures and Tables

Summary

High youth unemployment in the Middle East and North Africa (MENA) region is broadly recognized as one of the key catalysts of the Arab Spring, and of its accompanying period of political, social, and economic upheaval. With an unprecedented share of the population of the region now in early working age due to the timing of the "demographic bulge," the youth unemployment crisis appears set to plague the region for years to come in the absence of offsetting policy.

In this study, we conducted 13 focus groups with six to eight participants each and 14 one-on-one qualitative interviews to examine the perceptions of young Jordanian men and women (ages 15–30) on issues relevant to their transitions into adult roles, including aspirations for work and family, perceptions toward fairness in the labor market and barriers to employment, and attitudes toward the government as well as political and civic participation. Participants came from the largest city and the nation's capital, Amman, as well as the less urbanized nearby area of Zarqa. The findings from focus groups and interviews are placed into perspective through a literature review and secondary data analysis of national statistics, as well as interviews with country and topic experts.

Despite strong economic growth in the new millennium, unemployment in Jordan remains stubbornly high, and labor force participation markedly low. Youth labor force participation is under 30 percent, and it is very low among young women (11 percent); for working-age women overall it is only 17 percent. Unemployment among youth (at 30 percent) is almost double that of the overall working-age population. Persistent high unemployment is paradoxical in the context of robust economic growth in Jordan—growth that moreover has created jobs. Several factors appear to explain this paradox. First, the growth primarily occurred in construction and manufacturing subsectors (especially garments) characterized by low-paying jobs, with new positions largely filled by foreign workers. Earlier research suggests that unemployed Jordanians are not willing to take the jobs that are being created because of high reservation wages and the nature of the work, and that there is a strong preference for work in the public sector.

The education system in Jordan has undergone rapid growth in the past few decades, although concerns about quality remain. On internationally standardized tests, students in Jordan do not fare as well as counterparts in other countries at similar income levels, although students in Jordan tend to perform better than those in other Arab countries. Consulted experts cite a number of problems with the preparation of young graduates. These experts note that young people lack both the appropriate academic focus and the broad range of noncognitive skills—language, teamwork, problem solving, and so on—that are considered important for work, particularly in the private sector. Furthermore, youth in universities are not choosing courses of study that provide necessary skills, instead focusing on social sciences and humanities, as well as certain specific professions, such as medicine and law. This is particularly a problem for young women, who are encouraged (and possibly also prefer) to enroll in education, the arts, the humanities, and medical fields. Students who perform well on the secondary-school exit exam, the *tawjihi*, are expected by society and often pressured by their families to enroll in medicine, engineering, or law, irrespective of their own desires. On the other hand, those who perform poorly on the exam have permanently sealed off any chance of pursuing careers in those fields.

Facing poor economic prospects and inadequate income, youth are unable to marry, afford to live independently, or support a family. This stalled transition is also referred to as *waithood*; it is a time of relative inactivity and uncertainty, and it foments feelings of frustration and helplessness among youth that were evident in the focus groups and interviews. Furthermore, inability to fully participate in adult life is a form of social exclusion that is also economic in that, for example, someone who is not employed cannot get credit. Women in particular face a limited range of occupations as well as places of work that are considered acceptable to social expectations; discussions of these barriers emerged in the focus groups and interviews we conducted. The public sector, with large formal organizations, well-defined rules, and a lower likelihood of harassment, is generally more acceptable than smaller private firms, where there is less structure and hence (in the eyes of parents) less security and protection, in addition to more-personalized relationships. Thus, the lack of available jobs in the public sector tends to disproportionately affect women.

The focus groups and interviews with youth confirmed many of these patterns and provided additional insights. Key findings include the following:

- Not surprisingly in view of prior research, most youth would strongly prefer to work in the public sector, citing the job security and benefits that come with government positions. However, contrary to what one might infer from the literature, their expectations of achieving this goal do not seem to be unrealistically high. They understood that such jobs are now difficult to come by, and instead of holding unrealistic expectations, many simply expressed hopelessness at attaining good employment of any sort. They cited the low pay of available jobs, noting that salaries did not match the high cost of living.

- Regarding mismatch between what youth are taught and the skills they need for the labor market, youth participants themselves expressed concern over the lack of suitability of their educational preparation for the requirements of the job market. With respect to choice of career or subject of study, youth also stressed that they did not feel free in their career choices to pursue fields valued by the market, but instead felt pressure to conform to parental or societal expectations. Broadly, the focus groups give an impression that youth are aware of the deficiencies of the education system, lack of public sector jobs, and the far from ideal process of selection of professional paths, but feel unable to overcome the problems.

- Higher educational goals were very important to participants, and a very common refrain was that numerous obstacles prevented the attainment of these goals. These include the overriding importance for access to postsecondary schooling of achieving a high score on the secondary-school exit exam, as well as the financial costs of higher education.

- Some of the most interesting findings pertain to the situation of female youth. In contrast to statistics revealing very low female labor force participation in Jordan (including among young women), most female youth in our focus groups expressed their intentions to work. This suggests that low employment among this group ultimately does not derive from their having absorbed cultural or social views discouraging their economic participation, but rather from external barriers, whether these are from family or employers, or from other constraints, such as security. Also along these lines, a number of female participants stressed that their career choices were limited beyond the government sector—and within government were limited to a few professions, in particular teaching.

- With regards to broader life goals, considerable ambiguity or uncertainty was expressed about marriage. Young men did not lack the desire to marry, but rather conveyed uncertainty about their ability to support a wife and family, consistent with the literature on waithood. For their part, many women participants downplayed marriage as an important or, at least, immediate goal, in favor of pursuing a career. Again, our findings point to young women having considerable ambitions for career and independence, so that the constraints on achieving these outcomes seem to be largely external rather than internalized.

- Youth consistently expressed negative perceptions of the responsiveness of society and government to their needs and goals, and indicated that political parties did little to reach out to them. Participants in Zarqa voiced particularly high levels of hopelessness about the future, which is likely a reflection of the higher poverty and lack of economic opportunities in that region.

The findings point to a number of potential areas for policy change. Youths' reluctance to work in the private sector is contributing to unemployment problems and will also act to constrain the development of the private sector. This is compounded by inadequate preparation for such work in terms of skills, including both hard (cognitive) skills and soft (noncognitive) skills. Policies can address these problems in various ways. As many have already noted, school curricula at both secondary and postsecondary levels need to be reoriented to professions that will be more in demand (especially by the private sector), such as scientific and technical professions. Greater efforts can be made to encourage such careers, as well as to legitimize private sector careers and entrepreneurship more generally. Given entrenched attitudes toward certain careers, change may come slowly. Incentives can also be used—for example, by directing relatively more scholarships or financial aid to such areas of study.

However, the relative job insecurity and lack of benefits that orient youth preferences away from private sector work are real rather than merely a matter of attitudes or stigma. While the disparity in work hours, job security, and benefits between public and private sectors will not likely be eliminated, strong social safety nets and public support to the unemployed will serve to reduce risks incurred by those choosing private sector work. Both universal health insurance and unemployment insurance, if expanded and effectively implemented, might help expand the private sector labor market. Ultimately, however, strong growth in the private formal sector that leads to an increased supply of high-paying skilled jobs—which has generally been lacking—will be needed to attract and absorb growing numbers of new educated labor force entrants.

Both our findings and prior literature also indicate that women face particular constraints in developing careers, despite decades of improvements in female education. Young women face labor market barriers in access to many career paths, and their career aspirations are often discouraged by their parents. Because of these barriers, women seem especially poorly positioned to benefit from a growing private sector. Women have much lower participation than men in technical and vocational education training (TVET) programs, and this may reduce their ability to enter the labor market. While policy changes cannot alter the attitudes of employers (or parents) overnight, they can raise the benefits and reduce the cost of greater female access to work and to work-relevant study. Encouragement and provision of financial incentives for girls to study in nontraditional areas, such as science and technology, or (for those with less education) TVET programs should be increased. One approach to addressing this issue would be to combine training with measures that alleviate particular constraints to women's ability to work. This approach may have significant impacts, as seen in the successful efforts of the Jordanian Ministry of Labor to promote women's employment in Qualified Industrial Zones (QIZs) by providing free transport to work, subsidizing the cost of food in the zones, and subsidizing accommodations near factories. These policies helped overcome concerns about security and privacy. Similar measures could enhance more-educated women's participation in high-end occupations that remain largely closed to them.

The findings from this exploratory study lay the foundation for further analyses of youth aspirations and the labor market in Jordan. The goal of such analyses will be to develop more specific policy recommendations and levers to address the concerns of youth, build their human capital, and improve employment outcomes and hence life outcomes. It would also help sort out causal patterns and pathways behind youth behaviors to better tailor these policy levers.

Acknowledgments

The authors gratefully acknowledge a number of individuals who made this study possible and provided support throughout. We begin by thanking the International Middle East Youth panel that awarded the study authors the grant to conduct this work. We especially thank Center for Middle East Public Policy Director Dalia Dassa Kaye for her support and encouragement throughout the period that this study was undertaken. We thank Charlie Ries, vice president of international programs, for his support. We are grateful for the assistance of a number of people at various stages of this project, including Dana Torres-Rivas and Sharon Koga. We thank Nadine Khoury and the staff of the Market Research Organization, the Jordan-based survey research firm that conducted the interviews and focus groups, for their excellent work on this study.

The research greatly benefited from our interviews with expert consultants, and we thank the following individuals for their time and interest: Dr. Ragui Assad, University of Minnesota; Dr. Omar Razzaz, chair of the Board of Trustees, King Abdullah II Fund for Development, and chair of the Jordan Strategy Forum; Dr. Susan Razzaz, World Bank; Dr. Ibrahim Saif, minister of planning and international cooperation, Jordan; Dr. Edward Sayre, University of Southern Mississippi; and Dr. Musa Shteiwi, director, Center for Strategic Studies, University of Jordan.

We also had productive interviews with officials at the following organizations: Jordan River Foundation, Naseej Foundation, and King Abdullah II Fund for Development.

We also thank two reviewers for their very helpful comments and suggestions.

Finally, we are especially grateful to the youth who gave their time to participate in the interviews and focus groups.

Abbreviations

GDP   gross domestic product

ILO   International Labour Organization

IMF   International Monetary Fund

MENA   Middle East and North Africa

OECD   Organisation for Economic Co-operation and Development

PIRLS   Progress in International Reading Literacy Study

PISA   Programme for International Student Assessment

QIZ   Qualified Industrial Zone

TIMSS   Third International Mathematics and Science Study

TVET   technical and vocational education training

UNHCR   United Nations High Commissioner for Refugees

CHAPTER ONE

Introduction

High youth unemployment in the Middle East and North Africa (MENA) region is broadly recognized as one of the key catalysts of the Arab Spring, and of its accompanying period of political, social, and economic upheaval. Current unemployment of youth (ages 15–24)[1] hovers at around 25 percent, the highest among all regions of the world (World Bank, 2013). With an unprecedented share of the population of the region now in early working age due to the timing of the "demographic bulge," the unemployment crisis appears set to plague the region for years to come. This suggests that the confluence of concerns that brought about the Arab Spring is not going to be resolved in the short term and, in fact, may grow in importance.

The transitions to productive economic lives for young people in the region are stalled for numerous reasons: a gap between expectations of young people for well-paid formal or government jobs and limited supply of such jobs; education systems that fail to provide adequate levels of skills (confirmed by international tests) and the right kind of skills; slow economic growth and rigid policies toward business or the labor market that inhibit private sector employment; and finally the simple mathematics of the demographic bulge, which adds a large number of entrants to the labor force each year.

The economic costs of high youth unemployment are clear. Potentially just as serious are the social impacts, and these have specific policy resonance in the MENA context. For young men in particular, the inability to secure a livelihood prevents them from fulfilling their manifold adult social roles. For example, the lack of employment opportunities combined with the high cost of living (especially housing) appears to be delaying young men's ability to marry and have families. In this and other ways, economic exclusion leads to *social* exclusion. A sense of social exclusion will in turn, for many youth, reduce faith in existing social and democratic institutions and increase the appeal of violence and religious fundamentalism. It may also lead to self-destructive or health-risk behaviors, including drug use, which is rising quickly in the region (Shepard and DeJong, 2005).

Study Objectives

The purpose of this study is to examine the perceptions of young Jordanian men and women on issues relevant to their transitions into adult roles. We examine their aspirations for work and family as the key aspects of this transition. Success in these goals will be linked to their

---

[1] Unless otherwise noted, the statistical data from the World Bank and other external sources on youth refer to individuals who are 15–24 years old. However, our qualitative interviews and focus groups include youth ages 18–30, which is consistent with recent literature on this topic.

employment prospects, and thus we solicit their opinions of the adequacy of their preparation to join the labor market. We also examine their perceptions toward fairness in the labor market and barriers to employment. Finally, we examine attitudes toward political and civic participation, including the effectiveness and legitimacy of government and other institutions. We also examine the effects of stalled transitions to adult roles on the lives and behavior of Jordanian youth. To achieve the study objectives, we place these subjective perceptions into perspective through a literature review and secondary analysis of national statistics, as well as interviews with experts.

Interviews with Youth: Qualitative Data and Methods

We conducted focus groups and individual interviews with Jordanian youth sampled from Amman and Zarqa. Data collection involved using a semistructured interview guide focusing on six core topical areas: (1) problems facing Jordanian youth; (2) important goals for the future; (3) ideal jobs and job seeking; (4) educational experiences; (5) emigration from Jordan to other countries; and (6) youth empowerment and political participation. We used a purposive, stratified sampling strategy to maximize diversity across social class, age, neighborhood, and gender. Table 1.1 illustrates the distribution of participants across various demographic and sampling criteria.

We conducted 13 focus groups, each with six to eight participants. Focus groups were gender specific (eight male and five female groups), and efforts were made to have each com-

Table 1.1
Demographics of Participants

	Focus Groups	Interviews
Gender		
Male	8	9
Female	5	5
Area		
Amman	10	12
Zarqa	3	2
Age Group		
18–24	7	7
25–30	6	7
Social Class		
Impoverished but literate	3	2
Poor	2	2
Working class	4	7
Middle class	4	3

posed of individuals from a similar social class, with the range of classes represented in different focus groups. Assignment of social class relied on qualitative neighborhood and household information that was collected by a survey research organization based in Jordan. Three of the focus groups were classified as "impoverished but literate," two as "poor," four as "working class," and four as "middle class." The impoverished-but-literate focus groups were all recruited from Zarqa, while the remainder was recruited in Amman. Six focus groups were conducted with youth ages 25–30, and the remaining seven groups involved youth between 18 and 24.

We also conducted 14 one-on-one qualitative interviews (with nine males and five females). As with focus groups, this involved a mix of social classes (two impoverished but literate, two poor, seven working class, three middle class) and age ranges; seven interviews involved youth between 18 and 24 years of age, and the other seven involved youth between 25 and 30.

Interviews and focus groups were recorded and translated by interviewers, resulting in comprehensive notes containing verbatim quotes for each focus group and interview session. These documents (27 in all; 13 focus groups and 14 interviews) were imported into ATLAS.ti software for formal qualitative analysis.

Codes for qualitative analysis were developed with an iterative, team-based approach using inductive and deductive strategies (Bernard and Ryan, 2010)—that is, a mix of expected themes based on the interview protocol and existing literature, as well as new, unexpected themes arising from interview content. The core themes identified were (1) problems facing youth; (2) youth goals; (3) employment difficulties (including corruption, discrimination, etc.); (4) schooling and preparation for the labor market; (5) Jordanian social problems; (6) views of government and society (including discussions of the Arab Spring); (7) gender roles and restrictions; and (8) youth views on the future. The individual chapters to follow were informed by the results of the thematic coding as well as the existing literature and conversations with experts. For each chapter/subject, we pulled all of the relevant coded and subcoded material from each interview along with the attached demographic information and organized these data extracts in Excel spreadsheets. Reported themes and patterns for each section resulted from additional analysis (including counting subcoded material) in Excel.

Expert Interviews and Secondary Data Analysis

Conversations with subject and country experts were held on site in Jordan by two of the authors during a visit to Jordan, as well as via phone (to experts based in both Jordan and the United States). Experts included academic researchers and individuals involved in programming for youth, from a range of universities and nonprofit organizations, including the University of Jordan, World Bank, and Jordan River Foundation. Secondary data analysis involved a data download of the World Bank's Indicators database and a review of current reports from the International Monetary Fund (IMF), Organisation for Economic Co-operation and Development (OECD) Programme for International Student Assessment (PISA) database, and Third International Mathematics and Science Study (TIMSS).

Organization of the Report

The report is organized into five chapters. In Chapter Two we discuss the Jordanian economy and review basic labor market indicators. We draw from the focus groups to explore youth perceptions of their employment prospects, and the challenges and obstacles they face in the labor market. In Chapter Three we briefly review general education indicators, including progress and current challenges. We discuss findings from the focus groups and interviews on youth perceptions toward education as a means of achieving success in the labor market. We also discuss female perspectives on education opportunities and how these influence their employment prospects. In Chapter Four we examine general youth attitudes and aspirations, in particular the transition to adulthood, exploring young people's views on their ability to achieve financial independence, enter marriage and family formation, and engage in civic participation. Finally, in Chapter Five we conclude with a summary of our key findings and potential policy implications.

CHAPTER TWO

Economic Conditions and Employment

In this chapter we consider the Jordanian economy and the labor market, with a focus on Jordanians ages 15–30. The statistical data we cite from international sources such as the World Bank typically define youth as ages 15–24. However, our qualitative interviews and focus groups include youth ages 18–30, consistent with recent literature on this topic.[1] We review basic labor market indicators such as unemployment and labor force participation among youth and the working-age population in Jordan as a whole to provide a general context to the interview and focus group data. We also provide youths' perspectives on the employment situation in Jordan as well as their own job and career goals.

Labor and the Economy

The economy of Jordan, a small Middle Eastern nation of roughly 6.3 million people with few natural resources and an undeveloped industrial sector, heavily relies on aid, remittances from Jordanians working in other countries, services, and tourism. Some 10 percent of the Jordanian population lives and works in oil-rich Gulf States. At the same time, the Jordanian economy is heavily dependent on foreign labor, despite high and persistent unemployment among Jordanians themselves (13 percent for the working-age population). Some 300,000–400,000 nonrefugee foreigners work in Jordan, primarily in sectors such as construction and domestic labor.

Jordan is also a country with a long history of absorbing refugee populations. Palestinians fleeing the Arab-Israeli conflict were the first significant wave of refugees to cross the border into Jordan in the 1950s and 1960s. Today, Jordanian citizens of Palestinian origin are thought to make up more than half of the citizen population, although there are no officially published figures (Sharp, 2014). More recently, wars in Iraq in 2003 and now in Syria have brought in large influxes of refugees across the Jordanian border. The Office of the United Nations High Commissioner for Refugees (UNHCR) estimates that, as of 2013, more than 600,000 refugees reside in Jordan. Some 30,000 are Iraqi, and most of the remaining 500,000 registered or awaiting registration have fled from war-torn Syria (UNHCR, 2014; note the interviews

---

[1] Given the focus of this report on youth aspirations and labor market experiences, as well as to expedite the fieldwork, we chose to focus on the adult-age youth population (18 years and older) rather than 15 years and older. We also chose to include those over 24 years of age (up to age 30) to be more inclusive of youth and to capture the notion of delayed transitions or waithood, as reflected in the work of scholars who have looked at this issue specifically in the Middle East (Dhillon and Yousef, 2007; Dhillon et al., 2009).

and focus groups for this study were carried out before the Syrian refugee crisis significantly impacted Jordan).

Jordan has pursued market-oriented policies for more than two decades, and has done so more comprehensively than most countries in the region. Liberal economic reforms were started in 1989 by King Hussein and have been continued by his son King Abdullah since 1999. Among the policies that have been pursued are reductions in barriers to foreign investment, a significant privatization of the state's open enterprises, creation of tax-free zones (Qualified Industrial Zones; QIZs) to promote exports, a bilateral free trade agreement with the United States signed in 2009, and information technology sector promotion. These policies appear to have been successful both in attracting foreign investment and leading to economic growth for most of 2000–2011 (see Figure 2.1). Real gross domestic product (GDP) grew on average by a robust 6 percent per year between 2000 and 2010 (or about 4 percent per capita per year; IMF, 2012), better than average for the region, and largely based on strong export growth as well as the construction sector. Growth slowed down in 2010 and 2011, around the time of the global financial crisis and events associated with the Arab Spring. Both foreign direct investment and revenues from tourism declined sharply in 2011.

The Jordanian economy has a highly developed banking and finance sector, with finance and insurance composing the largest sector of the economy—followed by government, transport and communications, and manufacturing (which has grown rapidly from a small base in 2000). The government remains the largest employer in the economy, currently absorbing about 35 percent of the total employment and 42 percent of nonfarm employment (IMF, 2012). In the first half of the decade starting in 2000, in line with the overall market orientation, the share of public employment in total employment fell slightly (Taghdisi-Rad, 2012), though this was largely reversed toward the end of the decade. The dominance of the government as an employer is similar to other countries throughout the Middle East region.

Figure 2.1
Jordan: GDP per Capita (Constant 2000 U.S. $)

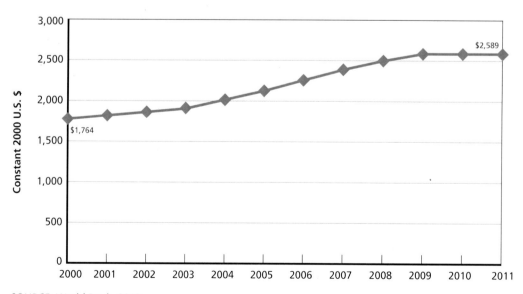

SOURCE: World Bank, 2013.
RAND *RR556-2.1*

Jordanian society and to some extent the Jordanian economy are characterized by the distinction between original "East Bank" Jordanians and the more recent Jordanians of Palestinian origin, who make up at least half of the population. East Bank Jordanians have traditionally had privileged access to employment in government and the military, and they have been politically dominant. As a consequence, Jordanians of Palestinian origin are more likely to be found in the private sector, including entrepreneurial activities.[2]

Youth Employment Outcomes

The literature review and interviews with expert informants point to several key factors that explain relatively high unemployment, especially for young people in Jordan. One such factor is unrealistic expectations for obtaining a government job at a time when most of the employment growth is occurring in the private sector. The second is a skills mismatch, which appears to be a region-wide phenomenon. Surveys of employers in the region suggest that secondary and postsecondary graduates are generally deemed not to have the necessary skills to ensure a smooth transition into the workforce, including soft skills (interpersonal, problem solving, teamwork), foreign language capabilities, and technical skills (Mourshed, Farrell, and Barton, 2012; PricewaterhouseCoopers, 2009). We discuss findings from the literature and expert interviews and follow that with a discussion of our findings from qualitative interviews and focus groups.

Despite economic growth in most of the first decade of the new millennium, unemployment in Jordan remains consistently high, and participation in the labor force is low. As of 2011, unemployment (the share of those in the labor force who are out of work and seeking work, as defined by the International Labour Organization [ILO]) in Jordan is 13 percent overall and is higher for women—21 percent, versus 11 percent for men (World Bank, 2013). Women's employment has remained very low in spite of very impressive improvements in education for girls in Jordan (as well as for boys). Females have not only reached parity in educational attainment with males but exceeded it, with higher female enrollments in both secondary and tertiary education.

Youth unemployment rates exceed adult rates by a wide margin, and the implications of high unemployment for youth are manifold, including concerns about consequences for political stability. While unemployment was 13 percent for adults overall in Jordan in 2011, it was 30 percent for youth ages 15–24 (Figure 2.2).[3] Fully half of the unemployed in Jordan are in this age group, among the highest shares globally. Unemployment is also highest among those with a bachelor's degree (Gurbuzer and Ozel, 2009). Higher unemployment rates of young women compared with young men suggest that those females who do enter the workforce face significant difficulties in getting hired. This may reflect discrimination in hiring as well

---

[2]   The distinction between East Banker and Palestinian may be relevant for the analysis of youth and labor markets as it implies potentially distinct opportunities and trajectories for young people in the two groups. However, while it would have been ideal to have a separate series of focus groups for each group, identifying geographical areas for recruitment that would clearly capture one or the other group was not straightforward, and within focus groups, it was felt to be too sensitive or potentially divisive to ask participants to identify themselves in ethnic terms and discuss disadvantages or privileges accruing to one or the other group.

[3]   Unemployment among young women is higher than young men: 47 percent versus 26 percent in 2011—though the figure for young men is itself very high (World Bank, 2013). It should be kept in mind that the absolute number of unemployed young women is much smaller than the number of unemployed young men, because so few young women are in the labor force to begin with (since unemployment is calculated only for those in the labor force).

Figure 2.2
Unemployment Overall and for Youth

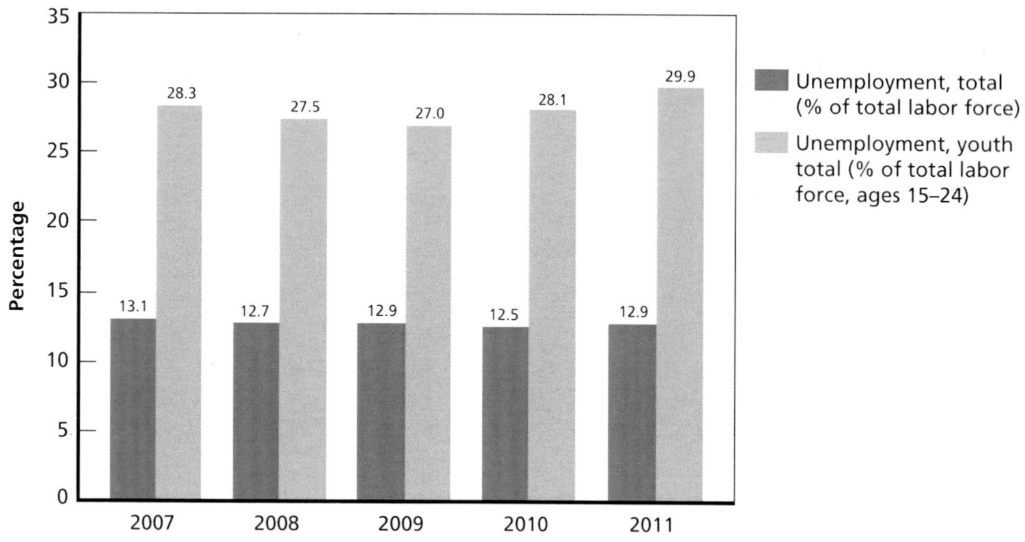

SOURCE: World Bank DataBank and authors' calculations.
RAND *RR556-2.2*

as restrictions on the types of jobs women seek due to social convention, constraints related to safety or travel, or their own preferences. Some studies have shown that a slowdown in the growth of public sector employment, as occurred in Jordan in the past decade, disproportionately affects women, given the social norms that prevent women from working in the private sector (Miles, 2002).[4] The low participation rate of young women (and women overall) itself points to such social (or other) barriers. Women may be discouraged from entering the labor market at all if they believe they will face discrimination in hiring or limits to the types of work deemed culturally acceptable, or due to family pressure.

Persistent high unemployment is paradoxical in the context of robust economic growth—growth that was creating jobs (World Bank, 2008). Several factors appear to explain this paradox. First, the growth primarily occurred in manufacturing (especially garments) and construction. These sectors are characterized by low-paying jobs, with the new positions largely filled by foreign workers. Between 2001 and 2005, an estimated 200,000 jobs were created, with almost two-thirds of those jobs filled by non-Jordanians (World Bank, 2008). Foreign workers (the bulk of them from Egypt) are generally willing to work for lower wages than Jordanians; further, employers are incentivized to hire foreign workers because, as they are on temporary contracts, employers do not have to contribute to social security or severance pay for these workers (Razzaz and Iqbal, 2008).

Research also suggests that unemployed Jordanians are not willing to take the jobs that are being created. Part of this clearly has to do with the wages being offered. Another factor is likely the nature of the work. In a survey of unemployed Jordanians looking for work, slightly

---

[4]   In contrast, focus groups and interviews with male and female youth suggest there is a perception among both men and women, albeit anecdotally, that a greater share of advertised vacancies target women rather than men. On the other hand, our review of research by the World Bank (2008) suggests that small businesses, in particular, have a strong preference against hiring women.

more than half indicated they would not work at wages offered for available jobs (Razzaz and Iqbal, 2008). Reasons for high reservation wages may include the ability to receive significant support from families that allows individual members to remain unemployed—including, importantly, support in the form of remittances from family working in the Gulf States—and a preference to work in, and wait for openings in, the public sector (Razzaz and Iqbal, 2008).

The expected rapid projected expansion of new labor force entrants in years to come could add to the unemployment problem under current trends in economic growth, with youth most seriously affected. Under the right conditions, Jordan could reap what is referred to as a demographic dividend, but it can also pose problems if the economy does not provide opportunities for these new entrants. Projections by the IMF indicate that under the assumption that the employment elasticity (change in employment per change in GDP) is unchanged, annual real GDP growth of 9.3 percent would be required to generate 0.8 million new jobs annually, the amount needed to absorb the projected growth in the labor force (IMF, 2012). This is well above the growth rate achieved even in the previous relatively high-growth decade. Concern over employment prospects of large numbers of new labor force entrants has led to a focus on labor market reforms and changes in education and training systems to improve employability of labor, as well as the development of the private sector to increase the growth of new jobs.

High unemployment rates in Jordan are combined with low labor force participation rates, defined as the share of the working-age population that is actually working or looking for work. The overall labor force participation rate (males and females together) is around 40 percent, with little change since the early 1990s.[5] Given unemployment, only about 35 percent of working-age people are actually employed, among the lowest in the world (IMF, 2012). Most notably, female participation is very low in Jordan, and indeed this is what pulls down the overall rate: it was 10 percent in 1990 and around 17 percent as of 2011. The youth labor force participation rate has remained under 30 percent since 1990.[6] The pattern of low female labor force participation is seen in many countries of the region, but it is particularly pronounced in Jordan.

In the following section, we draw from the interviews and focus groups with youth to explore their perspectives on employment and work, and the opportunities and challenges they face as they look toward transitioning to adulthood.

Focus Group and Interview Findings: Youth Perceptions of Employment Opportunities

As noted, recent growth in the Jordanian economy has been driven by the private sector, in keeping with the government's overall market-oriented stance. Previously, secondary and university graduates (particularly if they were East Bank Jordanians and not of Palestinian origin)

---

[5] Unless otherwise noted, statistics on participation, employment, and unemployment in Jordan come from the online World Bank DataBank, http://databank.worldbank.org/data/home.aspx.

[6] Male youth participation rates actually declined slightly, from 46 percent in 1990 to 42 percent in 2011. Female youth labor force participation rates rose slightly, from 7 percent in 1990 to 11 percent in 2011. For younger youth, ages 15–19, the data show almost no females in the labor force, compared with 21 percent of males. Participation rates for both are higher in the 20- to 24-year-old age range but are still only 18 percent for women, compared with 68 percent for men. These gender differences are maintained at older ages: among all females older than 15, 16 percent are in the labor force, compared with 66 percent of all males.

enjoyed almost guaranteed employment in the public sector. In the words of one of the experts we consulted, this "social contract" no longer holds.[7] Experts suggest that young job seekers tend to value employment in the government for its job security, relatively short working hours, and substantial nonwage benefits (typically lifelong pension and social security benefits). If the private sector were offering higher salaries, young postsecondary graduates might still prefer a government job. Hence, both aspirations and skills of youth are poorly aligned with the demands of the private sector, which is the main source of new jobs.

In focus groups and interviews carried out for this study, participants' comments underscored the idea of a strong preference for public sector jobs, citing benefits and job security. For example, one participant in a focus group of women ages 25–30 from a middle-class neighborhood in Amman was willing to forgo much higher pay in the private sector for the benefits of government employment:

> Previously, I used to work in a private company, and I used to earn double what I am earning right now. However, as soon as I got the public sector job I left the private sector. The public sector has a lot of benefits, like social security, and your children might get scholarships later on.

Two participants from a focus group of men ages 25–30 from a middle-class neighborhood in Amman echoed this sentiment:

> It's [a public sector job] a secure job for you and your children. There are a lot of benefits, *makroma*,[8] social security, health insurance.

> They [my family] believe that working in the public sector is better. I got a job in the Ministry of Education; they all blamed me when I didn't take it, not only my direct family but also my extended family. They think the public sector [has] the security.

Experts we interviewed indicated that postsecondary graduates, despite a lack of public sector jobs for youth, continue to expect a guaranteed government job; in other words, youth employment expectations and reality are disconnected. However, while there was a pronounced preference for public sector employment, youth in our focus groups did not appear to hold such illusions about their chances of getting such work; participants generally acknowledged that it was difficult to secure a government job today.

The fact that private sector jobs do not guarantee the same benefits that government jobs do is one clear disadvantage to such work for youth. Beyond this, however, there is also a negative social stigma attached to much private sector work, including self-employment and work in certain sectors, such as construction, which involve physical labor. This culture of shame, which is much talked and written about when discussion turns to youth in Jordan, may be a significant barrier to work among many young Jordanians.[9] The concept is used to explain

---

[7]   The gap between demand and supply of public sector jobs (though not specifically among secondary and tertiary graduates) is illustrated by data from 2007 indicating that the Civil Service Bureau received almost 180,000 job applications, of which 6 percent were hired (from Al Manar's 2010 Employment and Unemployment Survey, cited in Taghdisi-Rad 2102).

[8]   The word *makroma* in Arabic refers to something of noble quality or trait.

[9]   A *culture of shame* in this context refers to "the idea that certain types of work activities are dishonorable and that performing these jobs would lower one's social status" (World Bank 2008, p. ii).

the fact that certain sectors or subsectors of the economy are thoroughly dominated by foreign workers, including construction, which is also a sector that has experienced significant job growth.

Distinguishing between the culture of shame and simply inadequate pay or benefits as a reason why many youth stay out of the labor force is difficult, and would require further study to disentangle. However, youth appear reluctant to take work that does pay well if it has the undesirable characteristics just noted. Along these lines, recent research has shown that a substantial share of youth would rather not work (be voluntarily unemployed) than accept certain jobs at prevailing wages (World Bank, 2008). In focus groups and interviews, youth acknowledged that some jobs were considered undesirable by society, but that economic conditions at the time and the lack of more-desirable jobs are changing that perception. A female participant from a middle-class neighborhood in Amman in a focus group of ages 25–30 noted:

> Many Jordanian youth refuse to work in certain jobs like cleaning and that is why we are seeing a lot of expats here in Jordan working in those less desirable jobs.

> I would like to add something about the culture of shame; for example, Jordanian engineers refuse to work in certain jobs that you see Egyptians working in because they feel this is not prestigious enough for their standards and education, while they tend to forget that the Egyptian who decided to work here could also be an engineer in his country but was unable to find a job and had to work in any available job to get money.

It was also acknowledged that attitudes were changing. For example, in a male focus group (ages 25–30) in a middle-class neighborhood in Amman, one youth noted:

> But if you look back ten years, all the trashmen weren't Jordanian, but now they're all Jordanian. The way they look at them is different now.

> None of us would agree to work as [a] trashman, because we worked hard and got a higher education. But someone else wouldn't mind and there's nothing wrong with it. One of the things we need to get rid of is the shame. As I told you, I have engineering degree and I work as an electrician, but this is how I am securing my future.

Similarly, a male in a focus group for the younger cohort (18–24) from a middle-class neighborhood in Amman asserted:

> I personally worked as a painter (painting walls) when I was studying electric engineering in the university, and I do not think that this is wrong or shameful. I worked because I needed the money. I know a lot of university graduates right now who are working in restaurants and departments stores because they need the money.

However, it is important to note that while attitudes may be changing in general, the notion of a culture of shame remains an important factor in many youths' decisions to enter the labor force or not. This attitude was stated strongly by a male participant in a focus group of 25- to 30- year-olds from a poor neighborhood in Amman:

> If you come to me, and I don't have even enough food to eat, and told me to work as a garbageman, I would steal and become a thief and not become a garbageman. . . .

[My reaction is] because of the society, and how they look at someone who works as a garbageman! OK, there is disgrace when you work these jobs. The society will start to look at you differently. The society will automatically judge you if you work as a building guard or a garbageman. If you're sitting with some friends, and someone asked you what your job is, you'll feel very ashamed to say that you are a garbageman! Let's say you want to marry a girl, the first thing [her father] would ask me is about my job, and I would be in a very bad situation, because no one would give his daughter to a garbageman!

Patterns of high aspirations and lack of interest in certain forms of low-status (largely private sector) work are seen in other countries of the region, but they may be more prevalent in Jordan due to still-strong traditional views (particularly among East Bank or non-Palestinian Jordanians) that look askance at such work, and also the fact that strong tribal ties and extended families in Jordan allow youth to stay at home and not take undesirable work (Gorak-Sosnowska, 2009).

Youth, even university graduates, may choose to delay entering the labor force or accepting employment, because they are supported by their family or by remittances from relatives who are working abroad. Expert consultants describe these dynamics as recent trends, although limited hard data exist on their prevalence among the youth population. Youth unemployment in Jordan may be higher than would be expected for a country at its income level (all things being equal, lower incomes lead to less unemployment, as individuals have fewer options for support).

In discussions about how one secures a job, some focus group participants stated that *wasta* (connections through family or friends) is needed to secure a government job. According to some participants, *wasta* opened doors for people who otherwise did not meet the criteria for continuing into certain career fields at university, or for those who did not have access to wasta, meeting the criteria might not be sufficient. Other participants disagreed, claiming that wasta existed but was not as prevalent. In focus groups and interviews, greater emphasis was placed on the *tawjihi*, but having connections was deemed an important factor as well.[10] With respect to the private sector, consultations with experts revealed that personal connections, informal networks, and general word of mouth were how most job recruiting was done. Larger companies are more likely to recruit internationally and to use formal networks, such as job search sites, newspaper advertising, and career centers. Many of the most skilled young Jordanians are able to emigrate for work abroad, primarily in the Gulf States, while those remaining in Jordan are faced with declining prospects in the public sector and private sector jobs they do not want.

Youth not only perceive poor employment prospects; they also noted the high cost of living, which makes it difficult even for employed youth to transition into adult roles, so they delay marriage, starting a family, and purchasing a home. Among focus group participants

---

[10] The *tawjihi*, an Arabic term, is the mandatory national exam administered by the Jordanian Ministry of Education to all students in their final year of secondary school. It is required for graduation and entrance into public universities. It is also referred to as the stream or track that students pursue after entering secondary school. In Jordan, as is the case in most Arab countries, students either study science or literature. Focus group participants referred to *tawjihi* in terms of both the final examination and the stream (or track) of study.

who were employed, most cited low-paying jobs as a serious problem.[11] One male participant, 18–24 years old, from a middle-class neighborhood in Amman said:

> What I most don't like here in Jordan is high living standards and low wages. And when I say low wages, I'm not talking here only about the public sector but also about the private sector. Salaries in general here in Jordan are sometimes not enough for someone to survive every day and not only to live comfortably. The salaries of some people are not enough even to reach the end of the month, and so they start borrowing money from people and the financial pressure would for sure increase and their stress levels will increase knowing that they need to pay people back, and this is where the vicious cycle starts! I think that the country must take the low-wages problem into consideration and try hard to increase the minimum levels of salaries.

Male youth also discussed migration to other countries (namely the Gulf States) for better economic opportunities; a sizable number of Jordanians already work and reside in several countries of the Gulf. In general, among the youth focus group and interview participants who expressed a desire to migrate for work, individuals were about evenly divided between those who desired to leave Jordan permanently for better lives and those who wished to work abroad for a sufficient amount of time to save enough money to return and open their own businesses. The latter pattern represents a potential source of growth in the private economy and warrants further study.

Differences Between Female and Male Perceptions of Employment Opportunities

While the national data presented above reveal very low female participation in the workforce, most of the participants in the women's focus groups expressed an intention to work. For their part, male focus group members held a range of views toward the desirability of having a working spouse, varying from accepting it, and even considering it a desirable factor, to being completely opposed to it. On women's access to employment opportunities, male and female perspectives also tended to diverge. Some females viewed their employment opportunities as limited, while others, both male and female, noted an upward trend in demand for female job applicants. Participants based these observations on examination of vacancies posted in the local newspaper, and they cited telecommunications, retail sales, and administrative assistant positions as particular areas of growth in demand for female workers.

In this chapter we reviewed general economic and labor market indicators about our population of interest, Jordanian youth. We also drew from our focus groups and interviews to gain more-detailed insights into youth perceptions, views, and attitudes toward their employment prospects in Jordan. In the next chapter, we examine general education indicators in Jordan, in addition to youth perceptions of education opportunities and the role their education has played in building their human capital.

---

[11] Among focus group participants who volunteered information about their salaries, they reported salaries for secondary school graduates ranging from 150–300 Jordanian dinars (212–412 U.S. dollars) per month. A few participants reported higher salaries (400–500 Jordanian dinars, or 565–706 U.S. dollars per month).

CHAPTER THREE

Education Opportunities, Skills Mismatch, and Barriers to Completion

General Trends in Education in Jordan and the Region

Jordan's education system has experienced a truly impressive expansion over the last few decades. There is now universal or near-universal primary education (grades 1–6) enrollment and secondary education enrollment, which is comparable to OECD member countries. Post-secondary (or tertiary) education enrollment has generally remained steady over the past ten years, and is higher for women than it is for men. While Jordan's postsecondary enrollment is higher than other developing countries in the MENA region, it remains below OECD levels (Table 3.1).

Table 3.1.
Enrollment Indicators for Jordan, MENA, and OECD, 2005 and 2010 (%)

	2005			2010		
	Net Primary Enrollment	**Net Secondary Enrollment**	**Gross Tertiary Enrollment**	**Net Primary Enrollment**	**Net Secondary Enrollment**	**Gross Tertiary Enrollment**
Jordan	95.2	77.5	38.2	90.7	85.6	37.7
MENA (developing)	91.1	64.9	23.0	92.9	67.3	30.1
OECD	96.6	87.5	60.0	97.2	88.2	68.1

SOURCE: World Bank Indicators, 2013.

Although access to (or the quantity of) schooling has increased, the quality of the education being provided in Jordan and other Arab countries remains relatively low, as evidenced by student performance on internationally comparable standardized assessments. Students in Jordan did not fare as well as other countries at similar income levels, although students in Jordan tend to perform better than most other participating Arab countries. Girls also tended to outperform boys (OECD, 2010; Mullis et al., 2012; Martin et al., 2012).[1]

---

[1] Fifteen-year-old students in Jordan taking the PISA in 2009 ranked below OECD averages on reading, math, and science (OECD, 2010). Student achievement (eighth grade) on the TIMSS remained poor and went down from 1999 to 2011; see Chapter One of Mullis et al., 2012. In science, eighth-grade achievement, albeit below average, showed steady improve-

In a broad review of Jordan's education system and labor market needs, a 2012 World Bank report calls for a number of critical improvements to the education system, including upgrading and expanding schooling infrastructure to address overcrowding, improving rural and poor urban-area access to education, and enhancing vocational and technical education given the needs of the labor market for vocational skills (World Bank, 2012, p. 13).

Skills Mismatch

While the problem of the slow generation of well-paying private sector jobs cannot be discounted, lack of appropriate skills is clearly an important factor in high unemployment among university graduates in Jordan. In Jordan, as in other Arab countries, the types of high-status jobs in the private sector that are deemed desirable by graduates require higher-order skills that most graduates do not have. That is, there is evidence of a lack of coherence between the post-secondary schooling sector and business and industry needs.

Many observers have pointed to the shortcomings of the educational system in Jordan in terms of its ability to prepare young people for the labor market (World Bank, 2008; European Training Foundation, 2005; Ahmed, Guillaume, and Furceri, 2012). A broad consensus among experts we consulted was that young people lack both the appropriate academic focus and the broad range of noncognitive skills—language, teamwork, problem solving, and so on—that are considered important for work, particularly in the private sector. Employers in Jordan, as elsewhere in the region, cite lack of appropriate skills as an important constraint to hiring: 33 percent of firms in the World Bank Enterprise Survey cited this factor, broadly comparable to Lebanon (38 percent), Syria (36 percent), and Egypt (31 percent). The general perception among employers in Jordan and other Arab countries is that graduates of secondary and postsecondary institutions do not possess the requisite technical and soft skills, as well as the work ethic needed for the jobs that graduates expect to get (World Bank, 2008; Mourshed, Farrell, and Barton, 2012; PricewaterhouseCoopers, 2009).[2] Surveys of employers also report a dearth of skills in high-demand technical and vocational fields, with many resorting to importing labor to meet that demand.

With regard to academic focus, youth in universities are not choosing courses of study that are in relatively high demand in the labor market, instead focusing on the social sciences and humanities, as well as certain professions, such as medicine and law. This is particularly a problem for young women, who are encouraged, and possibly also prefer, to enroll in education, arts, humanities, and medical fields (World Bank, 2008). One expert consultant stated that postsecondary education was often pursued for its social status rather than for employment-related reasons.

---

ment from 1999 to 2007, but in the latest administration in 2011, students performed poorer than they did in 1999; see Chapter One of Martin et al., 2012.

[2]   Soft skills are skills such as teamwork, communication, and the general ability to work in a collaborative fashion. These types of skills are considered complementary to hard or knowledge-based skills and are increasingly essential in the workplace.

Focus Group and Interview Findings: Youth Perceptions of Education Opportunities

Focus group participants seemed to have an overall awareness of these problems. Participants pointed to a disconnection between what is taught in education institutions and what is required in the labor market. One female participant, age 18–24, from a middle-class neighborhood in Amman noted:

> If you look at the public education here, the student graduates from school, and then goes to university to study for four years, and then when he graduates, he faces the real world; the real employment life that has nothing to do with what he studied for the past four years in university.

Another female focus group participant among 25–30-year-olds from a middle-class neighborhood in Amman stated:

> I believe that there is a major problem in education. For example, when a student finishes the General Secondary Examination (*tawjihi*), there is no guidance as to what to do next. It is difficult for the student to establish his goal if he is not aware of what is next. He might end up choosing a certain field or specialization only to realize later on that this was not what he thought it would be. Later on, he will be shocked when he enters the labor market. Furthermore, there is also the problem of the salaries.

Returning to a general theme we have discussed, the economic liberalization and growth that Jordan has experienced over the past decade does not seem to have resulted in appreciable reductions in unemployment among Jordanians, especially among the youth population. A large part of the problem is that educated young Jordanians consider many of the jobs that are available to them (and which have been expanding in supply) to be undesirable (e.g., in construction), while they lack the skills (e.g., problem solving, critical thinking, and technical skills) required for the jobs they aspire to.

A recent assessment calls for stronger linkages between universities, on the one hand, and business and industry, on the other, to better align postsecondary curricula with the needs of the labor market (World Bank, 2012). The study also cites the need for greater university autonomy and control over governance to promote innovation and responsiveness to human capital needs (World Bank, 2012). Stronger connections of universities with industry and business could facilitate opportunities for career guidance and internships that impart relevant practical knowledge and experience to future graduates that will improve prospects for high-paying private sector work. These links could also promote leveraging private industry resources to institute improvements in the education system.

Drivers of Career Choice

Earlier we discussed the factors that affect youths' career choices, and in this section we discuss this issue in more detail. In our focus groups with youth, the most frequently mentioned and emphasized goal was to obtain a university degree, and many cited obtaining a doctoral degree as an ultimate objective. Focus group and interview responses, however, also suggest that career choices do not typically reflect youths' own desires. Participants instead cited familial and societal expectations as the driving force behind their career selections. In fact, a recurring theme was that career choices were driven less by market signals for desirable occupations than by youths' perceptions of parental and societal expectations. For example, participants stated that society valued certain professions, such as medicine, law, and engineering, over others. Some expressed feeling pressure to pursue those professions even if they had interests in other careers. One female participant in a focus group (ages 18–24) from a middle-class neighborhood in Amman summed up this notion:

> I was a good student with high grades during school, especially in math and physics. Anyhow, when I reached *tawjihi* level, I really wanted to join the literature section and not the science, but my mother was against it, and even the school principal was against the idea of me joining the literature section of *tawjihi* because I was good in science. But I really loved literature! The point is that here in Jordan, we have this discrimination problem, which is that those who are not that smart, or weak at school, are the ones to join the literature section, while the smart students are the one to join the science section! Again, what does this have to do with being smart or stupid? At the end it's the student choice, not the parents and not the teachers or school principal. Even my father was against the idea of me joining the literature section. He once told me that all your family members and relatives are studying science, and you're the only one to study literature, as if this is very shameful for him in front of the family and the relatives that his only daughter is studying *tawjihi* literature!

Constraints facing women are particularly strong. A number of female participants directly stated that their choices were limited beyond the government sector, or even beyond becoming a teacher. A female in a focus group (ages 25–30) from a middle-class neighborhood in Amman, when asked if it was difficult to find a desirable job, responded: "No, my problem has to do with my parents. They do not ask me what I want to do. I studied interior design but they do not allow me to work in engineering companies. I am only allowed to work as a teacher."

In one focus group of females ages 18–24 from a working-class neighborhood in Amman, there was an overall consensus on the constraints facing women (and men) in terms of career choice. All participants agreed with the following statements contributed by certain participants in response to questions about whether they faced pressure from parents and their interference in choice of a major:

> Yes, both us and males too.

> With girls' majors, yes.

> There are majors that are prohibited for a girl to study.

Another factor affecting career choice is performance on the secondary school exit exam, the *tawjihi*. Students entering secondary school (10th grade) choose between a science and a literature track. At the end of the final year of secondary school (12th grade), a high-stakes written assessment tailored to the track is administered, which students must pass to complete their secondary school education. In order to qualify for a career in medicine, engineering, or law, a university applicant must attain a score within a range that is centrally determined by the government's higher-education system. That score and, consequently, access to a certain field of study in the public postsecondary education system are almost exclusively determined by a student's performance on the *tawjihi*.[3] A low score on this exam is likely to have far-reaching implications in terms of postsecondary education pursuits, and thus future employment prospects. A number of youth expressed helplessness over getting good work because of their poor performance on the *tawjihi* exam.[4] One male, age 18–24, from a middle-class family in Amman stated:

> I think *tawjihi* is a problem here in Jordan; it determines the life of a person. There are a lot of smart people who would really be creative and successful in life, but for some reason failed in *tawjihi*, so this will determine their lives, and they will end up being unable to continue university and enter the real world. I think *tawjihi* is unfair. Not all people who graduate from university or schools are smart socially and know how to deal with people in real life and be successful in what they do. Most of our curriculum is just memorizing without really understanding what you're learning. If you memorized *tawjihi* well, then you will pass, but it doesn't mean that you can be successful in life.

Barriers to the Pursuit of Postsecondary Education

Some focus group participants cited financial obstacles to obtaining a postsecondary education, because they had to work during or soon after completing secondary school. Participants explained that if students did not gain admission to one of Jordan's public universities, they would need to finance their education at one of the private institutions, and this was infeasible for many. Thus, many are unable to continue with postsecondary study. Even public universities charge fees. Furthermore, some families expect their children to go to work after secondary school rather than continue their education. Youth emphasized logistical, financial, and other constraints to obtaining their desired educational or training goals. For example, a female in a middle-class focus group (ages 18–24) stated:

> I know that I'm going to face lots of difficulties to accomplish my goal. The first difficulty is how I am supposed to save money to be able to continue my studies. Honestly, this is my biggest fear. . . . I have lots of responsibilities toward my family; I have two brothers at the university and I help them with the tuition fees, also I help my mother, who is doing her Ph.D. . . . I need to live, need to buy food, and pay for my transportation. So at the end, how can I save money to continue my studies?

In this chapter we have provided a general overview of the Jordanian education system and examined youth perceptions of education opportunities and the factors that drive their choice of career. We next turn to an examination of the aspirations and frustrations of youth related to marriage, political and social participation, and future expectations.

---

[3]   Under a proposed new policy, the *tawjihi* will be limited to two main streams—academic and vocational—in contrast to the present division into five independent streams, including science and literature (as academic streams) as well as information techonolgy, Islamic law, and agriculture. The plan appears to be designed to encourage greater enrollment in vocational study. We thank an anonymous reviewer for noting this planned change in the *tawjihi* system to us.

[4]   The role of the secondary school exam to employment opportunities has also been explored in other research. See, for example, Egel and Salehi-Isfahani, 2010.

CHAPTER FOUR

Aspirations and Frustrations of Youth

Previous chapters have focused on education and the labor market, both of which are important mainstays of individual life-course development. But youth also have other important concerns and life goals—including goals regarding family formation and what might be considered more-existential goals related to life satisfaction and one's place in the world. The Middle East as a region (and Jordan specifically) is experiencing rapid changes along a wide variety of dimensions, many of which impact youths' experiences, frustrations, and expectations for the future. In this chapter, we cover gender and family formation, political participation, and related concerns of Jordanian youth, largely drawing on the focus group and interview findings.

Marriage

Observations of Jordan and other countries in the region in recent years have given rise to the notion of *waithood*, whereby youth (especially males) are stalled in their ability to transition to adult roles, including work, marriage, and family (Dhillon and Yousef, 2007; Singerman, 2007). Generally, the cause is perceived to be the lack of employment opportunities for young men. Without adequate income, they are unable to marry, afford to live independently, or support a family. It is not just a time of relative inactivity; it is also a time of uncertainty. The inability to fully participate in adult life is a form of social exclusion.

The mean age at marriage in Jordan in 2004 was 29 for males and 25 for females (United Nations, 2012). Only 43 percent of men ages 25–29 were married in 2004, compared with 65 percent in 1979 and 56 percent in 1994. This is consistent with the notion of waithood, or, rather, of its increasing importance, but it should be kept in mind that the rising age of marriage reflects a number of other trends, including modernization and changing social expectations, as well as increased duration of schooling. The share of men ages 25–29 who are married is lower in MENA than in other regions, and it has also fallen faster than elsewhere.

The perspectives of youth (especially males) on marriage in our sample are in accord with the notion of waithood. Male youth expressed ambivalence toward marriage, but this was mostly driven by their uncertainty about the economic environment and their own economic prospects. That is, many men stated that they wanted to get married, but structural conditions stand in the way of this goal. For example, one middle-class male (age 25–30) stated: "One should wait until he's 30 so he can get a good salary that will enable him to afford marriage expenses." Another male, categorized as "poor," from Amman (age 25–30) was considerably more frustrated and hopeless about his marriage prospects: "Without a job I have nothing!

I can't secure my future, I can't help my family, I can't get married. . . . Basically, I can't do anything! I have to get a job and make money to be able to achieve other goals in life." Along similar lines, a working-class male participant in a focus group (ages 25–30) said: "We're single and we barely survive. It's a good thing we're not married!"

Interestingly (and perhaps reflecting the pace of social change in Jordan), young women tended to reject, or at least deemphasize, marriage as an important goal or ambition, emphasizing self-improvement instead. For example, a working-class female from Amman (age 18–24) stated:

> My ambition of course is not to get married and have kids like any other Jordanian Muslim girl. My goals and ambitions are different. Ninety-five percent of females in Jordan seek to get married and build a family, even my mother who notices how much trouble I go through to achieve my goals always tries to convince me to stop working and just go get married. . . . My goal is to be something important, to help and give the community back and even on international level! At the same time, to improve myself and benefit from all the hard work, to improve myself educationally and professionally.

Some youth thought that expectations for women in general were starting to change in Jordan to reflect more of an acceptance of women continuing their education and delaying or even forgoing marriage. For example, a female participant in one of the working-class focus groups (ages 18–24) said:

> Some parents believe that their daughter has finished her education and there is nothing else for her to do or if their financial status doesn't allow her to continue, then yes she should get married. However, if she has a chance to further continue her studies and work in a decent job then no, she shouldn't get married.

Gender

For women in our sample, restrictions related to gender roles loomed particularly large. For example, a participant in a female focus group (ages 25–30) stated:

> As females in Jordanian society, we still do not leave our shells. The women here are still controlled by their fathers, brothers, husbands, and maybe even their own sons. Therefore, women are still not totally free in a sense, and I personally would love to have the freedom to make my own choices.

Similarly, a female (age 18–24) from a working-class neighborhood said:

> We are raised in a way that a male has full freedom, and a female should be very conservative, . . . etc. We live in a man's world, especially in Jordan. Males have the right to do whatever they want, and if they met a woman who is as strong as him, or as independent as him, they would not even consider talking to her because here males are used to the idea that females are weak and that males have the right to do whatever they want toward females and in other things as well.

In more traditional and conservative communities, women faced additional barriers to continuing to postsecondary education. One female focus group participant, age 18–24, from an impoverished neighborhood in Zarqa noted:

> From another point of view, there is the social aspect, where some families are against sending their female children to university. . . . Parents consider the social aspect not the financial. They don't like females to go to university, [so that they don't] mingle with males. There is a lot of intolerance toward this idea.

While some female participants noted difficulties in pursuing higher education, either because their families would not allow it or they were constrained to pursuing their education at institutions close by, most young women (all members of female focus groups and half of female interviewees) expressed a strong desire to continue their education.

With regard to the labor market, female participation, as noted earlier, is extraordinarily low in Jordan. Research has indicated that one reason for this is the limited range of occupations as well as places of work that are considered acceptable to society in general and to parents specifically. For example, information technology is a so-called acceptable profession, but the tourism industry is less acceptable for women, as are other occupations that similarly involve significant interaction with men who are strangers (European Training Foundation, 2011). The public sector, with large formal organizations, well-defined rules, and a lower likelihood of harassment, is considered more acceptable than smaller private firms, where there is less structure and, hence, in the eyes of parents, less security and protection as well as more personalized relationships. The extended hours of much private sector work also limits women's ability to participate. Finally, as one of the experts we interviewed stressed, an inadequate public transportation system also inhibits female participation due to concerns over security and women traveling on their own for extended commutes.

Interestingly, in the focus groups, many of these details did not arise spontaneously. However, these factors were generally reflected in the perceptions expressed by a number of female participants that their career choices were limited beyond the government sector and, specifically, teaching.

The feelings of young *men* about women working and their careers are also important, given that male attitudes will influence what many young women are able to do (and perhaps what they choose to do to the extent that having or not having a career affects a young woman's desirability as a mate). Male participants were in fact divided in their opinions on the desirability or appropriateness of having a wife who works. Those with a positive view tended to cite the helpfulness of a second income and a general preference for an educated spouse. Those against women working preferred having a spouse dedicated to domestic duties. Some male participants perceived that women had many more opportunities and that employers preferred to hire women. The latter view may reflect the situation in a limited number of industries where women do predominate, such as the garment sector in Jordan's QIZs.

Political Instability and Hopelessness

Youth articulated a wide range of idealized goals and aspirations, but at the same time, themes of potential (and real) barriers to these goals as well as fears about the future permeated youths' discussions of their future prospects. Youth voiced strong concern about the spreading political instability in the region and its impact on their economic prospects as well as security. For example, a middle-class male from Amman (age 18–24) said:

> My only concern in the future would be if something happened in our country like what is happening now in the neighboring countries. In this case, yes, I will have lots of concerns of how to take care of myself and my family.

Another youth from a male working-class focus group (ages 25–30) explained how crises in neighboring states affected economic prospects in Jordan:

> What is happening now in Egypt or in Syria has affected us a lot. And all this happened over one night. The prices raised, trades got affected, etc. . . . . What happened in Iraq affected us. Lots of Iraqi refugees came to Jordan, and the real estate prices rose over one night, which affected us a lot. Now we can't afford to buy a house; real estate prices are unbelievably high.

When asked about how responsive societal and governmental mechanisms are to their goals, needs, and fears, youth were almost universally negative in their responses. Participants stated that they did not know how to reach out to political parties or others in power, and that these parties and individuals did not reach out to youth. For example, a male (age 25–30) in a focus group stated: "No one listens to us. The officials somehow think that we are idiotic. We want to make changes, but nothing happens. We try to speak, but nothing happens. No one listens. In the house, parliament, they actually insult youth."

This frustration with existing structures extended to parents and other authority figures; for example, a female focus group participant from Amman (age 18–24) said: "No one respects us. No one knows where to go or who to turn to. Parents say, 'You're still young. You don't get it. You don't understand.'" Protest was also seen as ineffective, in part due to the entrenched power of existing authorities. To give an example, a participant in a male focus group (ages 18–24) from Amman, said: "If we protest, nothing will happen. The government doesn't do anything, so how can we?"

Youth from Zarqa voiced particularly high levels of hopelessness about the future, which perhaps is a reflection of the poverty and lack of economic opportunities in that region. For example, a male focus group participant (age 25–30) stated: "If, God forbids, I get married and I have children and I reach a point where I can't provide my family with what they want, I'd rather commit suicide than live and see our situation destruct rapidly."

Meanwhile, a group of females from Zarqa in another focus group (ages 18–24) collectively stated their hopelessness, responding to each other's comments in sequence:

> Our families wiped our objectives, and our . . . They broke us psychologically.

> A girl like me, with two kids and an incarcerated husband, what objectives and goals in life would she have?

> We don't think farther than tips of our noses.

> Other than cooking, there is no goal for me.

At least implicitly, the problem of waithood, or stalled transitions into adulthood, permeated the discussions during focus groups and interviews. Participants remained dependent on their families or on relatives working abroad and were unable to earn enough money to move on to the next phase of their lives—being financially independent, getting married, and beginning a family. In a conservative society such as Jordan, this has significant implications. With social expectations remaining conservative, transition into married and family life remains central. Delays in this transition can be a significant source of youth restlessness and discontent. Furthermore, youth in our focus groups and interviews cited low wages, high living costs, and a failure of society and civil institutions to respond to their needs. The interviews and focus groups further highlight the patterns of differences between major urban centers, such as Amman, and smaller cities in less urbanized and poorer areas, such as Zarqa. Participants from the latter seemed particularly critical and frustrated with their situation.

CHAPTER FIVE

Conclusions

This study uses original qualitative data (focus group discussions and interviews with youth) as well as expert interviews and secondary data to explore the situation of youth and the labor market in Jordan. The qualitative data generally confirm findings from prior, mostly quantitative, analyses while adding a number of new insights. As always in such studies, caution is needed, as the sample may not be representative of all youth, though the study made efforts to achieve a balanced sample in terms of socioeconomic status and location.

The focus groups reveal (not surprisingly in view of prior research) that most youth would strongly prefer work in the public sector, citing the job security and benefits that come with government positions. However, contrary to what one might infer from the literature, their expectations of achieving this goal do not seem to be unrealistically high. They understand that such jobs are now difficult to come by, and instead of holding unrealistic expectations, many simply expressed hopelessness at attaining good employment of any sort. They cited the low pay of available jobs, noting that salaries did not match the high cost of living.

Regarding the mismatch between what youth are taught and the skills they need for the labor market, which also is frequently noted in the literature, youth participants themselves expressed concern over the lack of suitability of their educational preparation for the requirements of the job market. Regarding choice of career or subject of study, youth also stressed that they did not feel free in their career choices to pursue fields valued by the market, but instead felt pressure to conform to parental or societal expectations. Broadly, the focus groups give an impression that youth are aware of the deficiencies of the education system, lack of public sector jobs, and the far-from-ideal process of selection of professional paths but feel unable to overcome these problems.

Higher educational goals were very important to participants, and a very common refrain was that numerous obstacles prevented the attainment of these goals. These obstacles include the overriding importance for access to postsecondary schooling of achieving a high score on the secondary school exit exam, as well as the financial costs of higher education.

Some of the most interesting findings pertain to situation of female youth. While national statistics reveal very low female labor force participation even among young women, most young women in our focus groups expressed their intentions to work. This suggests that low employment among this group ultimately does not derive from absorbed cultural or social views discouraging women's economic participation; low employment rather comes from external barriers—from families, employers, or other constraints, such as security. Also along these lines, a number of female participants stressed that their career choices were limited beyond the government sector—and within government were limited to specific professions, namely teaching.

With regard to broader life goals, considerable ambiguity was expressed about marriage. In the case of young men, this seemed to have to do not with a lack of desire to marry but instead with uncertainly about their ability to support a wife, consistent with the literature on waithood. What is perhaps more interesting is the tendency of the women to downplay marriage as an important or, at least, immediate goal, in favor of pursuing a career. Again, our findings point to young women having considerable ambition for career and independence, so that the constraints to achieving these outcomes seem to be largely external rather than internal.

Youth consistently expressed negative perceptions of the responsiveness of society and government to their needs and goals, and indicated that political parties did little to reach out to them. Finally, expressions of general hopelessness about the future were common refrains among both male and female youth from the lower-income region (Zarqa) included in the sample.

Policy Implications

These findings point to a number of potential areas for policy change. Youths' reluctance to work in the private sector appears to be contributing to unemployment problems and may also act to constrain the development of the sector. This reluctance is paired with the problem of inadequate preparation for such work in terms of skills, including both hard (cognitive) skills and soft (noncognitive) skills. Policies can address these problems in various ways. School curricula at both secondary and postsecondary levels need to be reoriented to professions that will be more in demand, especially by the private sector, such as scientific and technical professions. Greater efforts can be made to encourage such careers and to legitimize private sector careers in addition to entrepreneurship generally. Given entrenched attitudes toward certain careers, change may come slowly. Incentives can also be used—for example, directing relatively more scholarships or financial aid to such areas of study.

Nevertheless, the relative job insecurity and lack of benefits that shape youth preferences away from private sector work are real, so these preferences are not merely a matter of attitudes or stigma. While the disparity in hours of work, job security, and benefits between public and private sectors are not likely to be eliminated, strong social safety nets and public support to the unemployed will serve to reduce risks incurred by choosing private sector work. In fact, Jordan already has well-developed social insurance programs by regional standards; the nation spends more than 25 percent of GDP on human development, education, health, pensions, and social safety nets, and about 7.5 percent of GDP on the health care system alone (World Bank, 2013). Some 80 percent of the population in 2010 was covered by public or private health insurance (Ajlouni, 2011). The national health care policy is directed at ensuring coverage of the poor, and the government is considering a universal health insurance scheme (UNDP, 2013). Further, in September 2011, the social security system introduced an expanded unemployment-insurance scheme.

Both universal health insurance and unemployment insurance, if expanded and effectively implemented, may help the operation of labor markets, in particular by encouraging younger workers to enter the private sector, as these schemes lower the risks to well-being from losing one's job. Ultimately, however, strong growth in the private formal sector that leads to an increased supply of high-paying, skilled jobs will be needed to attract and absorb growing numbers of new, educated labor force entrants.

The findings also confirm the particular constraints that young women face in developing careers, despite decades of improvements in female education. They face labor market barriers in access to many careers as well as discouragement from parents. Because of these barriers, women seem in a particularly poor position to benefit from a growing private sector. Women have much lower participation than men in technical and vocational education training (TVET) programs, which, together with less practical academic courses in regular education, may reduce women's ability to enter the labor market (UNDP, 2013).

While policy cannot change the attitudes of employers (or parents) overnight, it can raise the benefits and reduce the cost of greater female access to work and to work-relevant study. Encouragement and provision of financial incentives for girls to study in nontraditional areas such as science and technology—or, for those with less education, TVET programs—should be increased. Employers in nontraditional fields and in the private sector may respond to incentives to hire women—for example, tax breaks. However, a recent randomized study of a program for female community college graduates by the World Bank points to potential limitations of this strategy (Groh et al., 2012). The study tested (separately and together) the effects of a voucher for employers to subsidize young female hires for six months, and a 45-hour employability (soft skills) training course. The job voucher indeed led to substantially higher employment rates relative to controls, but apparently the effect is only temporary, while the soft skills training had at best weak effects outside of Amman. As the authors note, more-comprehensive policies to address female access and unemployment are needed.

A comprehensive policy approach would combine training with measures that alleviate particular constraints to women's ability to work. These measures may have significant impacts, as seen in the successful efforts of the Jordanian Ministry of Labor to promote women's employment in QIZs by providing free transport to work, subsidizing the cost of food in the zones, and subsidizing accommodations near factories. These policies helped overcome concerns about security and privacy. Similar measures could enhance the participation of well-educated women in high-level occupations that remain largely closed to them.

Directions for Further Research

The findings from this exploratory study lay the foundation for further analyses of youth aspirations and the labor market in Jordan. The goal of such analyses will be to develop more-specific policy recommendations and levers to address the concerns of youth, build their human capital, and improve employment outcomes and life outcomes that are contingent on having decent employment. It would also help sort out causal patterns and pathways behind youth behaviors to better tailor these policy levers. One approach is to carry out a nationally representative survey of youth. Recently (2012–2013) the ILO and the Jordanian government conducted such a survey, known as the School-to-Work Transition Survey, addressing a number of important issues raised in the current study, including perceptions of schooling adequacy, job-search activities, and obstacles to finding work.[1] Complementary research based

---

[1]   See the survey at the ILO's website: www.ilo.org/beirut/projects/WCMS_213477/lang--en/index.htm. This study is ongoing.

on the present findings could take several forms and be tightly focused on potential policy solutions. For both male and (perhaps especially) female youth, more information is needed on financial, social, and parental constraints placed on career and job choices. For example, this study suggests that young women are interested in work and career but are held back by external (parental or social) factors. Surveys or in-depth interviews with young women and with parents (and spouses) would illuminate the specific factors—e.g., security concerns and interactions with men at work—that are limiting young women's access to work, and what kind of measures would allay these concerns. For example, parents may lack awareness of current labor market realities and where opportunities for their children, including girls, are strongest. Research is also needed to further explore youth attitudes and constraints regarding private sector work and entrepreneurship, to determine the mix of policies, including social insurance measures, information campaigns, and incentives to youth or employers, that would result in more hiring in the private sector or more skills training oriented toward specific sectors.

The ideal methodological approach to these questions is a mixed methods strategy, combining a representative structured quantitative survey with in-depth qualitative interviews on a small subsample of youth and parents in the survey. The quantitative survey is necessary to capture regional and social variation in constraints and perceptions, such as between rural and urban youth. Qualitative interviewing, as in the present study, will permit a deeper and more-nuanced understanding of these factors.

Regarding skills gaps, surveys can also be used to provide objective measures of skills related to employability, including both cognitive and noncognitive or soft skills, through direct assessments carried out in the context of household-based surveys.[2] This would also provide important information on the distribution of skill shortfalls across different segments of the youth population—for example, secondary and tertiary graduates, males and females, and rural and urban youth. Finally, a complementary direction would be to conduct surveys of enterprises to understand the demand for and gaps in specific job skills; such surveys could further be used to explore how firms in the private sector can be engaged in policies for incentivizing the participation and hiring of youth, especially young women.

---

[2]   The World Bank's STEP Skills Measurement Study, carried out in eight countries, is advancing this approach through the development of standardized, and hence comparable, core instruments for measuring skills.

References

Ahmed, M., D. Guillaume, and D. Furceri. 2012. "Youth Unemployment in the MENA Region: Determinants and Challenges." International Monetary Fund. As of December 24, 2013: http://www.imf.org/external/np/vc/2012/061312.htm

Ajlouni, M. 2011. *Health Systems Profile (Updated): Hashemite Kingdom of Jordan*. World Health Organization.

Bernard, H. R., and G. W. Ryan. 2010. *Analyzing Qualitative Data: Systematic Approaches*. Thousand Oaks, Calif.: Corwin.

Dhillon, N., D. Salehi-Isfahani, P. Dyer, T. Yousef, A. Fahmy, and M. Kraetsch. 2009. *Missed by the Boom, Hurt by the Bust: Making Markets Work for Young People in the Middle East*. Middle East Youth Initiative Report. Washington, D.C.: Brookings Wolfensohn Center for Development/Dubai School of Government.

Dhillon, N., and T. Yousef. 2007. *Inclusion: Meeting the 100 Million Youth Challenge*. Middle East Youth Initiative Report. Washington, D.C.: Brookings Wolfensohn Center for Development/Dubai School of Government.

Egel, D., and D. Salehi-Isfahani. 2010. "Youth Transitions to Employment and Marriage in Iran: Evidence from the School to Work Transition Survey." Economic Research Forum. *Middle East Development Journal*, Vol. 2, No. 1, pp. 89–120.

European Training Foundation. 2005. *Unemployment in Jordan*. As of December 24, 2013: http://www.etf.europa.eu/pubmgmt.nsf/(getAttachment)/4E4904B283AC4CAAC12570E0003D00E7/$File/NOTE6KCEZX.pdf

———. 2011. *Women and Work in Jordan: Tourism and ICT Sectors; A Case Study*. Ed. Outi Kärkkäinen. As of April 15: http://www.etf.europa.eu/webatt.nsf/0/BE3D52C73C5D0031C12578CC0056B2DA/$file/Women%20and%20work%20in%20Jordan%20-%202011_EN.pdf

Gorak-Sosnowska, K. 2009. *Studies on Youth Policies in the Mediterranean Partner Countries*. EuroMed Youth III Program, European Union. As of April 8, 2014: http://www.salto-youth.net/downloads/4-17-1866/04-EuroMedJeunesse-Etude_JORDAN-090325.pdf

Groh, M., N. Krishnan, D. McKenzie, and T. Vishwanath. 2012. "Soft Skills or Hard Cash? What Works for Female Employment in Jordan?" Working paper, World Bank. As of April 8, 2014: http://documents.worldbank.org/curated/en/2012/10/16866089/soft-skills-or-hard-cash-works-female-employment-jordan

Gurbuzer, L. Y., and M. H. Ozel. 2009. "Youth Employment in the Hashemite Kingdom of Jordan: Characteristics and Determinants." Unpublished manuscript, Pantheon-Sorbonne University and International Labour Organization.

IMF (International Monetary Fund). 2012. *Jordan: Selected Issues*. IMF Country Report No. 12/120. As of December 24, 2013: http://www.imf.org/external/pubs/ft/scr/2012/cr12120.pdf

Martin, M. O., I. V. S. Mullis, P. Foy, and G. M. Stanco. 2012. *TIMSS 2011 International Results in Science*. Chestnut Hill, Mass.: TIMSS and PIRLS International Study Center, Boston College. As of April 8, 2014: http://timssandpirls.bc.edu/timss2011/international-results-science.html

Miles, R. 2002. "Employment and Unemployment in Jordan: The Importance of the Gender System." *World Development*, Vol., 30, No. 3, pp. 413–427.

Mourshed, M., D. Farrell, and D. Barton. 2012. *Education to Employment: Designing a System That Works.* McKinsey Center for Government. As of April 14, 2014: http://mckinseyonsociety.com/downloads/reports/Education/Education-to-Employment_FINAL.pdf

Mullis, I. V. S., M. O. Martin, P. Foy, and A. Arora. 2012. *TIMSS 2011 International Results in Mathematics.* Chestnut Hill, Mass.: TIMSS and PIRLS International Study Center, Boston College. As of April 8, 2014: http://timssandpirls.bc.edu/timss2011/international-results-mathematics.html

OECD. 2010. *PISA 2009 Results: Executive Summary.* As of April 8, 2014: http://www.oecd.org/pisa/pisaproducts/46619703.pdf

PricewaterhouseCoopers. 2009. *Arab Human Capital Challenge: The Voice of CEOs.* As of April 8, 2014: http://www.pwc.com/m1/en/publications/arab-human-capital-challenge.jhtml

Razzaz, S., and F. Iqbal. 2008. "Job Growth Without Unemployment Reduction: The Experience of Jordan." Unpublished manuscript, World Bank.

Sharp, J. 2104. *Jordan: Background and U.S. Relations.* United States Congressional Research Service, RL33546. As of April 8, 2014: http://www.refworld.org/docid/5301e9e64.html

Shepard, B. L., and J. L. DeJong. 2005. *Breaking the Silence: Young People's Sexual and Reproductive Health in the Arab States and Iran.* Boston: Harvard School of Public Health.

Singerman, D. 2007. "The Economic Imperatives of Marriage." Working paper, Brookings Wolfensohn Center for Development/Dubai School of Government.

Taghdisi-Rad, S. 2012. "Macroeconomic Policies and Employment in Jordan: Tackling the Paradox of Job-Poor Growth." Employment working paper no. 118, ILO, Employment Policy Department, Geneva.

UNDP (United Nations Development Programme). 2013. *Jordan Poverty Reduction Strategy: Final Report.* As of December 24, 2013: http://www.undp.org/content/dam/jordan/docs/Poverty/Jordanpovertyreductionstrategy.pdf

UNHCR (Office of the United Nations High Commissioner for Refugees). 2014. "Jordan: 2014 UNHCR Country Operations Profile." As of February 18, 2014: http://www.unhcr.org/pages/49e486566.html

United Nations. 2012. *World Marriage Data 2012.* As of April 8, 2014: http://www.un.org/esa/population/publications/WMD2012/MainFrame.html

World Bank. 2008. *Hashemite Kingdom of Jordan: Resolving Jordan's Labor Market Paradox of Concurrent Economic Growth and High Unemployment.* Report no. 39201-JO.

———. 2012. *Country Partnership Strategy for the Hashemite Kingdom of Jordan for the Period FY12–FY15.* International Bank for Reconstruction and Development and International Finance Corporation.

———. 2013. "Jordan." As of April 8, 2014: http://www.worldbank.org/en/country/jordan/overview